COUNTRIES IN OUR WORLD

PAKISTAN

Andrew Langley

FRANKLIN WATTS
LONDON•SYDNEY

First published in 2010 by
Franklin Watts
338 Euston Road
London NW1 3BH

Franklin Watts Australia
Level 17/207 Kent Street
Sydney NSW 2000

Produced for Franklin Watts by
White-Thomson Publishing Ltd
+44 (0) 845 362 8240
www.wtpub.co.uk

Series consultant: Rob Bowden
Editor: Sonya Newland
Designer: Amy Sparks
Picture researcher: Amy Sparks

A CIP catalogue record for this book is available
from the British Library.

Dewey Classification: 954.9'1053

ISBN 978 0 7496 9199 8

Printed in Malaysia

Franklin Watts is a division of Hachette
Children's Books, an Hachette UK company.

www.hachette.co.uk

Picture Credits
Corbis: 1 (Ed Kashi), 5 (Jane Sweeney/JAI), 6 (Arshad
Arbab/epa), 8 (Ed Kashi), 12 (Matiullah Achakzai/epa),
14 (Ashley Cooper), 16 (Naeem Ul Haq/epa), 19
(Annie Belt), 21 (Mian Khursheed/Reuters), 22 (F.
Ahmed/epa), 24 (Bettmann), 26 (Rahat Dar/epa),
28 (Bennett Dean/Eye Ubiquitous); **Dreamstime:**
18 (Nasirnisar), 29 (Cyberlot); **Fotolia:** 9 (Marco
Gabbin); **Getty:** 7 (Tim Graham); **iStock:** 20 (Danish
Khan), 23 (Zoltan Kovacs); **Photoshot:** 17 (World
Pictures); **Shutterstock:** 11 (EML), 13 (Pichugin
Dmitry); **UN Photo:** 10 (Evan Schneider), 15 (Luke
Powell), 25 (Christopher Herwig), 27 (M. Grant).

Contents

Pakistan lies in South Asia, on the north-west side of the Indian subcontinent. It contains a huge variety of landscapes and peoples, with many different cultures, languages and lifestyles.

The Land of the Pure

Pakistan is one of the largest Islamic countries in the world. Its name in Urdu, the language spoken in Pakistan, means 'Land of the Pure'. Troubled relations with its neighbours, Afghanistan to the west and India to the east, over land ownership have led to long periods of unrest and conflict in Pakistan. These problems have made life difficult for the Pakistani people, and have stopped the country developing politically and economically.

▼ *Pakistan is bordered by Iran, Afghanistan, China and India. To the south, it has a stretch of coastline along the Arabian Sea.*

The birth of Pakistan

The area that is now Pakistan used to be part of India, which was ruled for many years by the British. When India became independent in 1947, the Muslims there demanded their own homeland. The new nation of Pakistan was created for the Muslims, leaving the rest of India to stay mainly Hindu. Originally Pakistan was in two parts, made up of a western section (the present-day country) and an eastern section on the Bay of Bengal. In 1971, the eastern part broke away and became the country of Bangladesh.

Crossroads of the world

Pakistan occupies a key position in the world, which has had a huge effect on its history. It lies on the important east-west trade link through the Khyber Pass between Europe and Central Asia. The Indus Valley is also a natural route from the north to the warm waters of the Indian Ocean. This has made Pakistan a vital crossroads, used by armies, traders and migrating peoples for many centuries.

▼ *The Khyber Pass is a 53-km (33-mile) mountain pass that links Pakistan and its neighbour Afghanistan.*

IT STARTED HERE

The Indus civilization

About 5,000 years ago, a great civilization grew up in the valley of the Indus River, which runs through Pakistan. Its people built some of the world's first cities, including Harappa and Mohenjo-Daro. The buildings were made of mud-brick and stone, and had drains and water-storage tanks. The Indus people also developed an early system of writing.

Terrorism from Pakistan?

Pakistan lies at the centre of one of the most troubled regions of the world. These difficulties have been made worse in recent years because of the rise of Islamic terrorism. After the attacks on the USA on 11 September 2001, the USA and its allies – including the UK – started their 'War on Terror' by invading Afghanistan. The Pakistani government helped them in this fight against the Taliban and other violent groups. But the Pakistani army has struggled to control the regions near the Afghan border, where many terrorists have strongholds.

BASIC DATA

Official name: **Islamic Republic of Pakistan**

Capital: **Islamabad**

Size: **803,940 sq km (310,403 sq miles)**

Population: **176,242,949**

Currency: **Pakistani rupee**

▼ *Groups of armed rebels called militants carry out attacks because they are angry at government arrests. Here they have blown up a police car near Peshawar.*

Pakistan today

The long period of violence has stopped Pakistan's economy growing as quickly as it might. It is a relatively poor country and much of its population lives in poverty. Despite this, some experts believe that Pakistan has the potential to change the situation, and predict that it will become one of the world's largest economies in the twenty-first century. The violence has also weakened Pakistan's government – it has been difficult or impossible to keep control of some areas, and this has resulted in poor relations with neighbouring countries. However, Pakistan enjoys good relations with powerful countries like the USA and China.

▲ *The growth of busy, modern cities such as Islamabad suggests that Pakistan has the potential for economic development.*

GOING GLOBAL

Pakistan has been named as one of the Next Eleven (N-11) countries. These are 11 nations that are believed to have great potential for development over the next few years, and that are predicted to become powerful economies. The other N-11 nations are Bangladesh, Indonesia, Iran, Vietnam, Turkey, Egypt, Mexico, Nigeria, South Korea and the Philippines.

Pakistan has three main kinds of landscape. High mountain ranges cover most of the north and west of the country. To the east are low-lying plains, watered by the Indus River. There are dry desert areas on each side of the plains.

River of life

The Indus River is the most important water source in Pakistan. With a total length of 2,900 km (1,800 miles), it runs right through the country, from the northern mountains to the Arabian Sea in the south. Farmers on the plains channel water from the Indus to help grow their crops. The river provides a vital supply of drinking water to Pakistan's population. The Indus also runs through part of north-west India, and it has been at the centre of disputes between Pakistan and India over water use.

IT'S A FACT!

Every year, the summer heat causes snow and ice in the high mountains to melt. The water drains into the Indus River, making the water level rise. Between July and September, the river often overflows its banks and floods the plains of Punjab and Sind. For thousands of years, farmers in the region have used the flood water to irrigate their crops.

▼ *A family of fishermen prepare their nets on the banks of the Indus River.*

THE HOME OF...

K2

The mountain called K2 lies on the northern border between Pakistan and China. It is the second highest peak in the world, after Mount Everest, reaching 8,611 m (28,251 ft) above sea level. It has been nicknamed the Savage Mountain because it is so difficult to climb.

▲ *Only around 300 people have successfully climbed K2, which stands on the border between Pakistan and China.*

Pakistan's climate

The different landscapes of Pakistan have different climates. The high mountain regions have warm summers and very cold winters. The Punjab Plain in the middle of the country is the hottest area, with temperatures reaching more than 45°C (113°F) in summer. Pakistan is a very dry country, with an average of only 25 cm (10 in) of rain a year. Rainfall varies widely throughout the land, and most rain falls during the summer monsoon. The wettest region is eastern Punjab, while the driest is the Baluchistan plateau in the south-west.

▲ *Rescue workers search for survivors in the wreckage of a school after the 2005 earthquake.*

Damaging the environment

Like other parts of the world, Pakistan faces major threats to its natural environment. Huge areas of forest in the north have been cut down, and this has increased the risk of flooding. These floods not only drown people and damage buildings, they also erode (wear away) valuable soil and help spread diseases such as cholera and dysentery, which are carried in the water.

IT'S A FACT!

Earth tremors are common in the mountains of northern Pakistan. Sometimes, these are severe earthquakes that cause widespread damage and death. In 2005, one of the deadliest quakes of all time killed at least 75,000 people in the Azad Kashmir area. The disaster sparked a massive international rescue effort. Relief workers, with vital supplies and equipment, arrived from all over the world.

Pollution problems

There are even bigger threats to the quality of Pakistan's water and air. Factories and textile mills produce waste that poisons the water, and farmers are using more and more pesticides and chemical fertilizers. These pollute lakes and rivers, and often make water unfit to drink. Because there are few laws about vehicle emissions, a typical Pakistani car or lorry releases up to 25 times more dangerous gases than those in the USA or Europe.

Wildlife in danger

With its many different kinds of landscape, Pakistan is home to a huge variety of wildlife, including crocodiles, bears, eagles and wild cats. But today many of these are threatened, largely because of pollution and hunting. Among creatures in great danger are the rare snow leopard and the Asiatic black bear. Some of these are now protected in game reserves to try to increase their numbers.

◀ *There are fewer than 450 endangered snow leopards now left in Pakistan.*

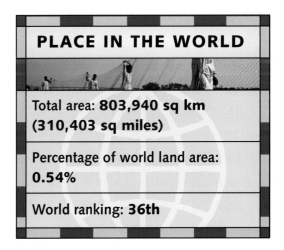

PLACE IN THE WORLD

Total area: 803,940 sq km
(310,403 sq miles)

Percentage of world land area:
0.54%

World ranking: 36th

Population and migration

Pakistan has the sixth largest population in the world. More than two-thirds of its people live in small villages. The most heavily populated areas are the plains along the Indus Valley, and the far south of the country.

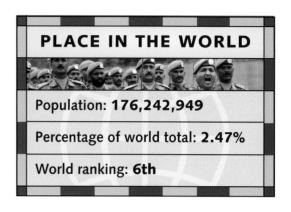

PLACE IN THE WORLD

Population: **176,242,949**

Percentage of world total: **2.47%**

World ranking: **6th**

The people of Pakistan

There are six major ethnic groups in Pakistan. The largest is the Punjabis, who make up 44 per cent of the total. Punjabis have traditionally taken a leading role in government and the armed forces. The next largest groups are the Pashtuns (15 per cent), who live mainly in the northern part of the country, and the Sindhis (14 per cent), who live mainly in Sind province. Other big groups are the Sariaki (eight per cent) and the Balochi (three per cent). Muslims who came to Pakistan from India after independence are called Muhagirs, and they make up seven per cent.

◀ The Pashtun are the second largest ethnic group in Pakistan. They are concentrated near Afghanistan, and members of the tribe live on both sides of the border.

Major cities

Karachi, on the Arabian Sea coast, is by far the biggest city in Pakistan. When it was chosen as Pakistan's first capital in 1947, its population was about 400,000. Today the total has risen to at least 12 million, and it is still growing quickly. Karachi is also the country's main port, and the centre of finance and industry. Since 1960, however, the newly built city of Islamabad in the north has been the Pakistani capital. Other large cities include Lahore, Faisalabad and Rawalpindi, which are all in Punjab province.

▲ *Brightly coloured local buses in Karachi, the largest city in Pakistan, and once the country's capital.*

IT'S A FACT!

Pakistan's population is growing at a rate of two per cent a year. This places it 57th in the world table – far above the USA (0.88 per cent), the UK (0.28 per cent) and Germany (-0.04 per cent).

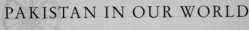

▲ *A Pakistani corner shop in Lancashire, UK. There are Pakistani communities in many Western countries.*

GOING GLOBAL

Number of Pakistanis living abroad: 3,973,549

Major emigrant destinations:

Saudi Arabia	1.1 million
UK	0.9 million
United Arab Emirates	0.5 million
USA	0.2 million
Canada	0.2 million

Pakistanis around the world

When the nation of Pakistan was established in 1947, it was a very poor country. Few people could find work and many lived in poverty. Over the next 50 years, huge numbers of Pakistanis emigrated to other countries in search of a better quality of life. There are now large populations of Pakistanis in the UK, the USA, Canada and other countries. Today, nearly four million Pakistanis live overseas. About three million of these are in Middle Eastern countries. Coney Island in New York and Bradford in England are home to well-known Pakistani communities.

Emigrant wealth

Pakistani workers overseas still have a big impact on their native land. Many of them send regular payments of the money they have earned to their families back in Pakistan. In early 2009, these payments – known as remittances – reached over US$700 million a month, which makes a huge difference to the lives of many people in Pakistan. Some emigrant business people have also invested in industrial and other projects within Pakistan. This money and investment has helped Pakistan's economy and the people who live there.

Refugees from Afghanistan

Over the past 40 years, Pakistan's neighbour Afghanistan has suffered from civil war and invasion by other countries, most recently US-led forces as part of the 'War on Terror'. There are still thousands of American and United Nations troops in Afghanistan. Since the 1970s, more than five million Afghan refugees have fled to Pakistan. Most of them settled in the north-west of the country near the border. The Pakistani government and international aid agencies have helped some return home, but there are still many Afghan refugees in Pakistan. In total, there are believed to be more than two million foreign refugees in Pakistan – more than in any other country in the world.

IT'S A FACT!

The average life expectancy at birth for Pakistanis is 63 years for men and 66 for women, which is one of the lowest in the world. In comparison, the life expectancy for people living in the European Union is 76 for men and 82 for women; in the USA it is 75 for men and 81 for women.

▼ *The Roghani refugee camp is situated in Chaman, a Pakistani border town. Afghan children and young people make up a large percentage of the camp's population.*

Throughout its long history, many different peoples have settled in the region that is now Pakistan. Modern Pakistani society is made up of a variety of cultures, and each one has its own customs and lifestyle.

Language

All the different cultures in Pakistan are reflected in the many languages spoken throughout the country. Urdu is the official language, but is commonly spoken by fewer than one in 10 of the population. English is widely spoken too, especially by members of the government and the armed forces. More than half of the population speaks Punjabi or Siraiki (which is very similar). The other main regional languages are Sindhi, Pashtu and Balochi.

▶ *English is widely spoken in Pakistan, and the English versions of books such as Harry Potter are sold there.*

FAMOUS PAKISTANI

Nusrat Fateh Ali Khan (1948–97)

Nusrat was a Pakistani singer and songwriter who became famous in both Asia and the West. His work was based on the traditional music of the Sufis (an Islamic movement). Nusrat's passionate singing in concerts and on record made him a giant of world music.

Religion

Many Pakistanis feel more loyal towards their own cultural group than to society as a whole. This makes it difficult to create a truly united Pakistani nation. However, religion is one thing that unites Pakistani people no matter what their background or ethnic group. The vast majority of Pakistanis (96 per cent) are Muslims. Most of these are Sunni Muslims, though some are Shiite. Pakistan is also home to small numbers of Christians, Hindus and members of other religions.

THE HOME OF...

Shah Jahan mosque

The Shah Jahan mosque in Thatta, near Karachi, is one of the most beautiful buildings in the world. Built of brick and decorated with coloured tiles, it covers an area of nearly 4,700 sq m (50,590 sq ft). Its 93 domes produce such a perfect echo that prayers said in one part of the mosque can be heard everywhere.

▼ *The Shah Jahan mosque was built by the emperor for the people of Thatta in 1644.*

Family life

Family is very important to Pakistanis. Many people live together in extended family groups, which include grandparents, parents and children. The oldest man is usually the leader and is responsible for taking care of his family. Traditionally parents chose who their children would marry, but these traditions are slowly changing, especially in the cities, where television, the Internet and rising living standards have opened up Pakistan to influences from other parts of the world.

GLOBAL LEADER

Cricket

Pakistan is one of the world's leading international cricket teams. Its side won the cricket World Cup in 1992, and was runner-up in the first World Twenty20 competition in 2007. In early 2009, Pakistan ranked as the fifth highest Test-playing nation in the world.

▼ *Pakistani cricketer Khurram Manzoor bats against Zimbabwe. Pakistanis are passionate players and fans of the game.*

Children and education

Pakistani children go to school from the age of five, and can go on to secondary school at 15. Schooling is one area where girls have gained some equality in recent years. Traditionally, girls received very little education, but the number of girls going to primary and secondary schools has increased since the 1990s. Even so, female literacy rates are low. Only about 36 per cent of women over 15 can read and write, compared with 63 per cent of men.

◀ *Boys read in their classroom. Although more girls are learning to read and write, they still lag behind boys because very few girls attend school.*

The role of women

In many parts of Pakistan, women still have traditional roles within their family. They are responsible for keeping the family's honour, so their social freedom is limited. Many have little contact with men outside their family, and spend most of their time in the home. In farming areas in the countryside, women live more freely because they have to work in the fields. Increasingly, Pakistani women are challenging these old ways, and have formed movements to fight for equal rights.

IT'S A FACT!

Alcohol is forbidden under Islamic law, but Pakistanis have a wide choice of refreshing drinks to take with food or to keep them cool. Tea is the most popular, including a green tea called *kahwah*, flavoured with saffron and other spices. Other favourites are sugarcane juice, *lassi* (a milky yoghurt drink), and *gola ganda* (a sweetened water ice).

Economy and trade

Pakistan's economy and standards of living have improved since the country was established in 1947. But in the last 10 years Pakistan has faced major economic problems. One cause is the unrest and violence created by the fight against terrorism. Another is the fall in money being invested by Pakistanis living abroad.

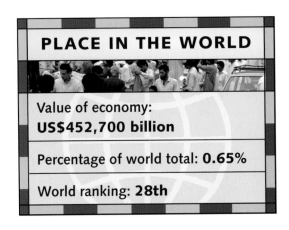

PLACE IN THE WORLD

Value of economy:
US$452,700 billion

Percentage of world total: **0.65%**

World ranking: **28th**

Farming

Agriculture was once Pakistan's most important industry and brought in more money than any other. Today, though, it makes up only 20 per cent of the value of all the goods produced in Pakistan. Even so, nearly half of Pakistan's workforce is employed in farming. The major food crops are wheat, rice, fruit and vegetables. Cotton and sugarcane are also grown as cash crops – crops that are grown especially to be sold rather than for farmers to use themselves.

▼ *Sindhi women working in the fields. While farming was once an important industry in Pakistan, it has been overtaken by the service industry.*

▲ *These people are collecting free mobile phones from the state-run phone company U-Phone in Islamabad. The communications industry is growing faster than any other in Pakistan.*

IT'S A FACT!

The Karakoram Highway between Pakistan and China is the highest paved road in the world. Parts of it are 4,693 m (15,397 ft) above sea level. The Highway runs for 1,300 km (780 miles) between Raikot in Pakistan and Kashgar in China. Completed in 1986, it has become an important trade route as well as one of Pakistan's biggest tourist attractions.

At your service

Today, service industries have taken over as the most important part of Pakistan's economy, earning over 50 per cent of the country's money. These industries include banking, insurance, and buying and selling goods. Transport is another major service. In a large country with many remote areas, the road, rail and air links are vitally important.

Manufacturing and mining

Factories process home-grown cotton to make textiles (cloth) and clothing, one of Pakistan's most valuable products. Clothes, shoes and sports equipment are also manufactured from leather. Other factory-made items include steel, chemicals and electrical goods. Pakistan has many natural resources, especially valuable minerals. The most important of these are oil, natural gas, coal and limestone, which is used to make cement.

▼ *Women making clothes in a factory in Quetta. Clothing and textiles are among Pakistan's most important exported goods.*

GLOBAL LEADER

Hydroelectricity

The Tarbela Dam on the Indus River contains one of the biggest hydroelectric power stations in the world. The mountainous northern part of Pakistan is ideal for harnessing the power of water. Over 20 per cent of the country's power is generated in this way. However, 40 per cent of Pakistani households have no access to electricity.

▲ *A drilling rig in northern Pakistan. The country's reserves of oil and natural gas are extremely important to its economy.*

Trading with the world

Pakistan sells its goods to many different countries. The USA is its biggest customer, taking 18 per cent of exports. The United Arab Emirates, Afghanistan, China and the UK also buy large quantities. In recent years, Pakistan has opened up new markets by signing free-trade agreements with some of its neighbours in South Asia and the Middle East, as well as with China.

The global slump

The economic crisis that began in 2008 affected most countries in the world and Pakistan suffered as much as any. Inflation caused prices to rise sharply, while the value of the Pakistani rupee fell. The government received big loans from the World Bank and the Asian Development Bank, and in November 2008 it borrowed US$7.6 billion from the International Monetary Fund. These loans helped to make Pakistan's economy more stable.

Pakistan is a democratic republic, which means that the people elect their own members of parliament, who in turn elect the president and prime minister. However, Pakistan's recent political history has been stormy and violent, and several politicians have been assassinated.

Leader and parliament

The president is the head of the Pakistani state, but the day-to-day running of the country is the job of the prime minister, who is head of the government. As in the UK and the USA, there are two houses of parliament, which are called the Senate and the National Assembly in Pakistan. Among the leading political parties are the Pakistan People's Party and the Pakistan Muslim League. Each province, or area, of Pakistan also has its own elected assembly.

FAMOUS PAKISTANI

Muhammad Ali Jinnah (1876–1948)

Jinnah was the inspiring leader of the campaign to found Pakistan as a separate Muslim nation. In 1947, he became the country's first governor-general. Jinnah is still celebrated as the 'Father of the Nation' and 'Great Leader', and his birthday is a national holiday in Pakistan.

▶ *Muhammad Ali Jinnah (right) – the father of the Pakistani nation – meets with Indian leader Pandit Jawaharlal Nehru in 1946.*

Military muscle

Pakistan's army, navy and air force make up one of the biggest armed forces in the world. In recent years they have been in action against Islamic terrorists in the northern tribal areas, and in Kashmir, a region being fought over by Pakistan and India. The armed forces have played a big part in Pakistan's history. In 1999, for example, the military leader General Pervez Musharraf seized power and, although he had not been elected, he remained the country's leader until he was forced to resign in 2008.

GOING GLOBAL

In 2001, the USA, the UK and other allies invaded Afghanistan, as part of the 'War on Terror'. The Pakistani government agreed to support the invaders, and allowed them to use three of its airfields. In return for this support, Pakistan received money and military equipment from the USA.

▼ *As part of the United Nations, Pakistani soldiers have joined peacekeeping missions in several countries. These Pakistani troops are on a mission in Liberia.*

Muslim militants

The biggest political problem in Pakistan today is violence in the remote mountain areas of the north. A militant form of Islam has grown up here, helped by the arrival of extremist fighters from nearby Afghanistan. Fighting between Pakistani forces and militants in 2009 caused huge numbers of people to flee to safety away from the mountain villages.

Clash in Kashmir

For over 50 years, Pakistan and India have argued over the Kashmir region, in the north-east. They both claim it belongs to them, and have gone to war three times. China also claims part of the region, and many people in Kashmir want it to become an independent state. In addition to this, both Pakistan and India developed nuclear weapons in the 1990s. This has increased the feeling of mistrust between the two countries.

◀ *Benazir Bhutto in 1995, when she was prime minister of Pakistan.*

FAMOUS PAKISTANI

Benazir Bhutto (1953–2007)

Bhutto was the daughter of Zulfikar Ali Bhutto, who led Pakistan in the 1970s. Benazir herself was elected prime minister twice, in 1988 and 1993, becoming the first woman leader of a Muslim country. After a period of exile, she returned to Pakistan in 2007, and was assassinated only days before a general election.

Human rights

Pakistan has had a poor record on human rights. Tribal unrest, long periods of military rule and police brutality have led to many abuses. Religious minorities have been persecuted and freedom of speech has been limited. However, there is now a growing movement for reform, led by Pakistan's Human Rights Commission. During 2008, there were major protests by lawyers when General Musharraf sacked senior judges.

▼ *Lawyers join a rally to protest against the sacking of judges in 2008.*

IT'S A FACT!

Pakistan is one of only nine countries to have nuclear weapons. Both Pakistan and India had been racing to develop nuclear weapons since the 1970s, and both countries successfully tested them in the 1990s. There is great international concern about this, as India and Pakistan have been enemies for many years, and there is a fear that they may use the weapons against each other.

Many people find it hard to see how Pakistan will recover in the next few years. The economy is still suffering, there is still a lot of fighting and unrest, and many people think Pakistan's leaders are not strong enough to solve the country's problems. But they will have to be solved before Pakistan can begin to make progress towards a fairer and more confident society.

Looking for peace

The first task will be to find a lasting settlement of the violent conflicts at home and in neighbouring Afghanistan. The USA and its allies are aiming to create stability in Afghanistan and then to withdraw. If this happens successfully, the border areas in northern Pakistan may also become more peaceful. At the same time, talks will continue with India to find a lasting agreement over the future of Kashmir, and it is a good sign that the ceasefire established in 2004 has been honoured.

▼ *Peaceful solutions to the conflicts in northern Pakistan will give children hope for a brighter future.*

Strong government

Pakistan has suffered from a series of weak or corrupt leaders, and from long periods of military rule. Strong leadership will restore the ordinary people's faith in their government. This will include reform of the legal system, a programme to bring greater equality between men and women, and resolving the tensions between Pakistan's different ethnic groups.

GOING GLOBAL

Modern communications are having a big impact on Pakistani society and its attitudes. Over 90 million people have mobile phones. New telephone and broadband networks are being built throughout the country. This has inspired a growing band of bloggers who feel free to express opinions that can be read all over the world.

◀ *Buildings like the Saudi-Pak Tower in the Blue Area of Islamabad – the city's business centre – reflect Pakistan's possibilities as a thriving commercial centre.*

Building up the economy

A more efficient government over the next 10 years may also speed up the economic recovery. The country has plenty of natural resources that will become increasingly valuable, including oil and natural gas. It also has a healthy and rapidly expanding service sector. Careful management and bigger investment could make Pakistan much wealthier, and if the country becomes more stable, its tourist industry may improve, bringing in much-needed money. Pakistan's presence on the list of Next Eleven countries is a good sign – it shows that other nations see its potential. International confidence in Pakistan could have a positive effect on the country.

Glossary

blogger someone who broadcasts a diary or commentary through a personal Internet website.

cash crop a crop grown especially to be sold, usually to another country, rather than for personal use.

civil war a war fought by two or more groups within the same country.

democracy a political system in which the government is elected by the people of the country.

economy the financial system of a country or region, including how much money is made from the production and sale of goods and services.

ethnic group a group of people who identify with each other and feel they share a history.

export to transport products or materials abroad for sale or trade.

extremist someone who holds extreme religious or political views, and who may resort to violence to get their point across.

Hinduism the religious faith of Hindus, based mainly in India.

hydroelectricity electricity generated by turbines that are turned by running water.

Islam the religious faith of Muslims, founded by the prophet Muhammad (peace be upon him).

life expectancy the average number of years lived by a country's population.

literacy the ability to read and write.

militant a group of unofficial soldiers, not part of a regular army, which fights strongly for a cause.

plateau a raised area of land, usually fairly flat and sometimes also called 'tableland'.

pollution spoiling the environment with man-made waste from factories, car exhausts, etc.

refugee someone who flees from war, oppression or persecution in search of refuge and safety.

republic a nation with an elected president as head of state, rather than a king or queen.

resources things that are available to use, often to help develop a country's economy. Resources could be minerals, workers (labour) or water.

subcontinent a large land mass that forms a distinct part of a continent, such as India.

terrorist someone who uses violence and terror to try to achieve their aims.

textiles cloth or fabric, usually made from weaving or knitting.

Urdu the official language of Pakistan.

Further information

Books

P Is for Pakistan (World Alphabet)
by Shazia Razzak
(Frances Lincoln, 2007)

Pakistan, the Culture (Lands, Peoples & Cultures)
by Carolyn Black
(Crabtree, 2002)

World in Focus: Pakistan
by Sally Morgan
(Wayland, 2007)

Changing World: Pakistan
by David Abbott
(Franklin Watts, 2010)

Discover Countries: Pakistan
by Geoffrey Barker
(Wayland, 2010)

Websites

www.cyberschoolbus.un.org
The United Nations information website on
countries of the world.

www.pakistan.gov.pk
Information about the different government
departments in Pakistan.

www.pcboard.com.pk/home.html
The official website of the Pakistan Cricket Board.

www.statpak.gov.pk
Facts and figures from the Pakistan government.

www.tourism.gov.pk
The official government tourism site.

*Every effort has been made by the publisher to ensure
that these websites contain no inappropriate or offensive
material. However, because of the nature of the Internet,
it is impossible to guarantee that the content of these sites
will not be altered. We strongly advise that Internet access
is supervised by a responsible adult.*

Index

Numbers in **bold** indicate pictures